LAUGH OUT LOUD

MORE KITTEN AROUND

Laugh it up, fuzzball!

By Jeffrey Burton

LITTLE SIMON
New York London Toronto Sydney New Delhi

LITTLE SIMON
An imprint of Simon & Schuster Children's Publishing Division
1230 Avenue of the Americas, New York, New York 10020
First Little Simon edition July 2017
Text copyright © 2017 by Simon & Schuster, Inc.
Photographs copyright © 2017 by Thinkstock. All rights reserved.
All rights reserved, including the right of reproduction in whole or in part in any form.
LITTLE SIMON is a registered trademark of Simon & Schuster, Inc., and associated colophon is a
trademark of Simon & Schuster, Inc.
For information about special discounts for bulk purchases, please contact Simon & Schuster Special Sales at
1-866-506-1949 or business@simonandschuster.com.
The Simon & Schuster Speakers Bureau can bring authors to your live event. For more information or to book an event
contact the Simon & Schuster Speakers Bureau at 1-866-248-3049 or visit our website at www.simonspeakers.com.
Designed by Brittany Naundorff
Manufactured in China 0517 QUL
10 9 8 7 6 5 4 3 2 1
ISBN 978-1-4814-9959-0 (pbk)
ISBN 978-1-4814-9960-6 (eBook)

Welcome and get ready to **LAUGH OUT LOUD** with this Animal Meme Joke Book that's out to prove once and for all that wildlife are the funniest critters on earth.

Before you start, here are some helpful tips to make this book even funnier:

- give each animal its own special voice
- give each joke its own special delivery
- make sure you share the best jokes with your friends
- and don't be afraid to make up your own jokes, too!

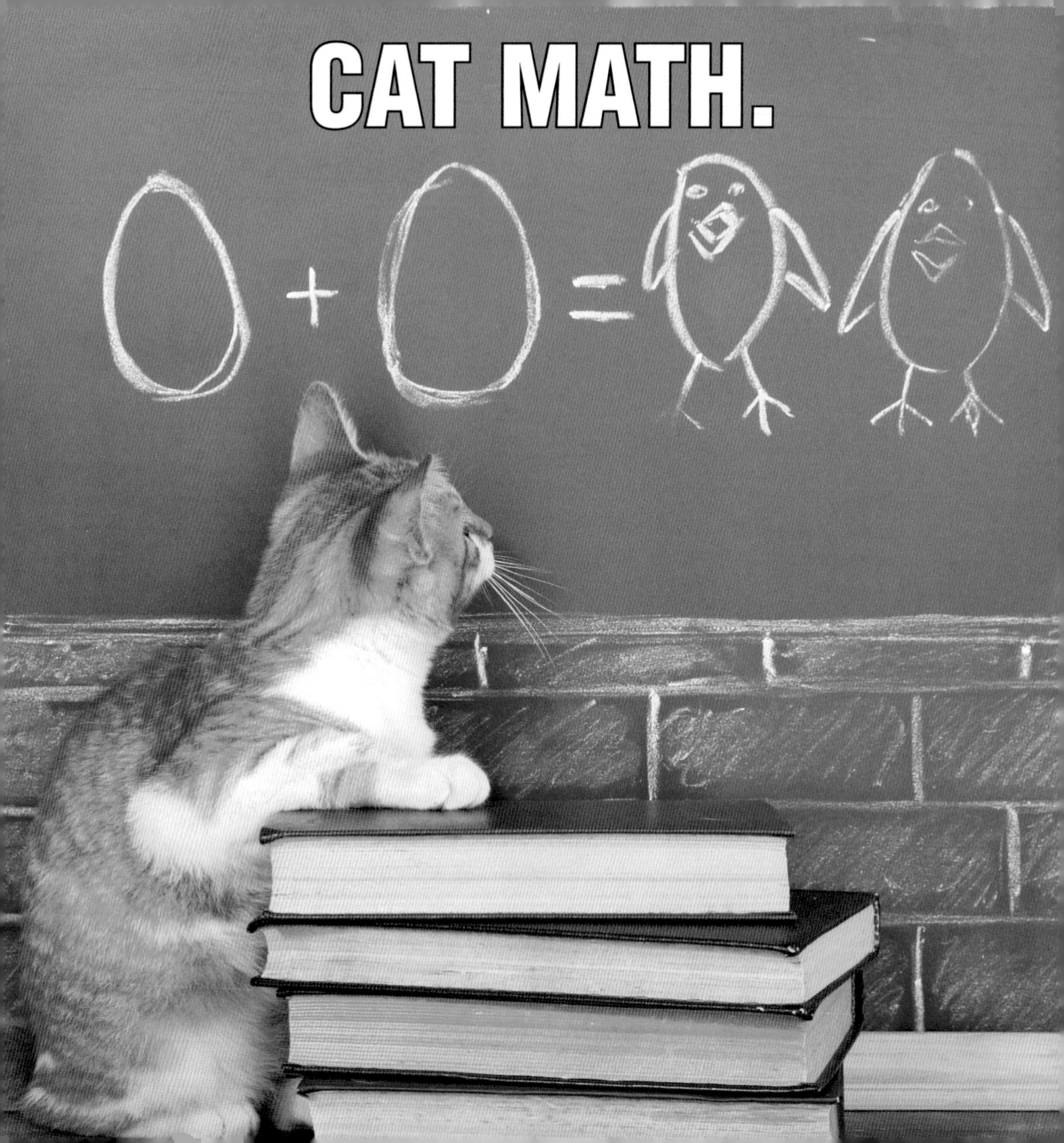
CAT MATH.

CHECK OUT MY LAMB CHOPS.

BUBBLE TROUBLE!

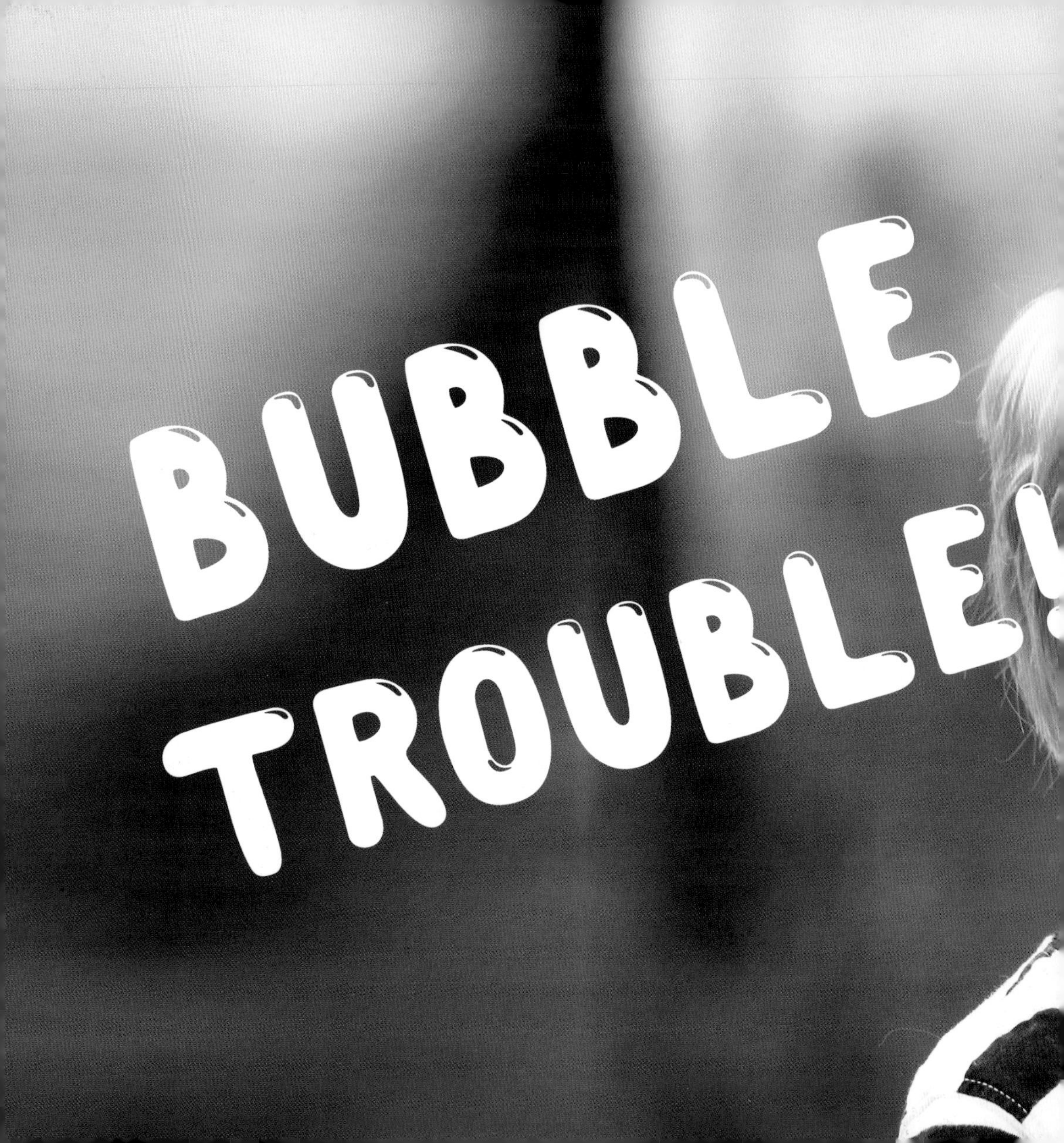

Real BUTTERfly kisses aRe horRifying!

DUH.

10 OUT OF 10 CATS AGREE:

They need to run to the next room for NO REASON.

(at all)

(like right now)

I swear they're Easter eggs. Stinky, colorful Easter eggs.

let's get quackin'!

In the jungle,

the mighty jungle,

the lion steps on a Lego.

BAD SELFIE.

I know **KARATE** and 100 other dangerous words.

flamin-goes

wheRever they
want to.

HELP! I'M TRAPPED IN AN INVISIBLE BOX!

SWAFK.
Sealed with a frog kiss.

YOU'RE DOING IT WRONG.

When dad tells a joke.

Okay, *now* I'm a little

COLD.

When someone's like,

PLEASE

PASS THE

CORN...

Only TOUCAN BEAK the

best you in the world!

MATH GOT ME LIKE.

WHEN YA GOTTA GO,
YA GOTTA GO.

TRUST ME, KID. YOU DON'T WANNA GO TO HORSE JAIL.

THIS GRASS IS MINE.

ALL MINE!

Video games count as homework, right?

OH NO! VACUUM!

Uhm, I have a Question!

MONKEY FACT:
Liars don't wear pants on fire.
(They don't wear pants at all.)

Cat dentist says, "I can see you've been *flossing*."

WEIRDEST. PIRATE. EVER.

WHEN YOUR PARENTS MAKE YOU SHARE A ROOM.

CHILL OUT,
I GOT THIS.

The majestic meow cow is

SPOTTED!

The trick is, you gotta

land on your feet!

DOG WISH YOU HERE.

CAT LEVITATION

THIS HAIR TASTES

SO GOOD!

HIGH PAW!

these aRen't the Right
PURRRRR-SCRIPtion.

YOU GOT THIS!

If you make a video of your dog, he'll think he's a movie star.

WHAT WAS IN THAT KIBBLE?

PRINCIPAL CAT SAYS GET BACK TO CLASS.

RIGHT MEOW!

ONE DOES NOT SIMPLY PICK UP THE CAT TOY
AND NOT PLAY WITH THE CAT.

BAD SELFIE.

I don't always pretend to be a cat,
but when I do,
I doo-doo in the litter box.

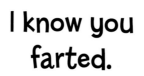

LIZARD
WIZARD!

And you thought cowlicks were bad—

Good evening. I'm Klaus, and I will be your dog butler.

May I fetch you something?

I'M HAIRY PUPPER.

BRAND-NEW COUCH, HERE I COME!

We're getting

a little

antsy.

Hello. I'll be your teacher this year and my class is gonna be . . .

Over here!

Aww, you brought me the treats?!

I thought this was

a dance PURR-rty.

this is not a dog.

I'M
INVISIBLE!

Hey? Where'd the water go?

CAT MISSION IMPOSSIBLE

oh.

weRe you
Reading that?

GOTCHA, HUMAN!

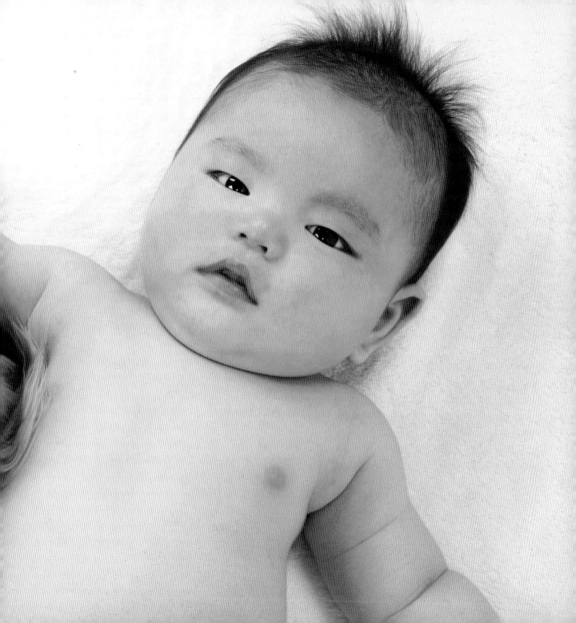

Hmmm, do I detect a note of rocky road ice cream on the floor?

What are those neighbors up to now?

HEY, PRIVACY, PLEASE?
I NEED A LITTLE ME-OW TIME.

HALF CAT. HALF BABY.

ALL CRAZY.

BAD HARE DAY.

i BELiEVE i CAN FLY!

THE PERFECT KID TRAP!

DID YOU HEAR THE ONE ABOUT THE BRAND-NEW TOY? I ATE IT.

Take my paw and I will lead you to the

SECRET CAT KINGDOM.

wanna hear something "bunny"?

SQUIRREL ON A SURFBOARD?!

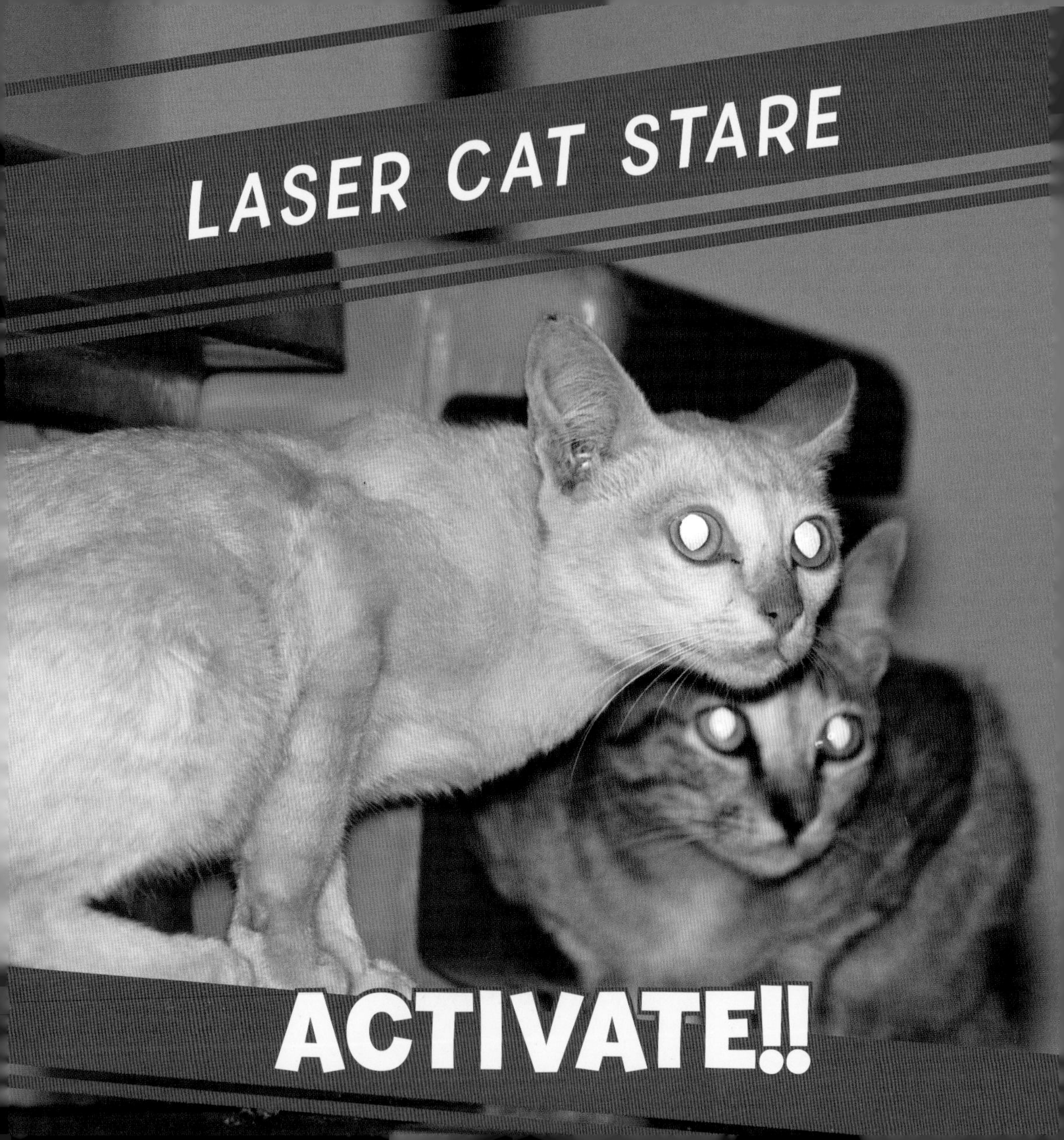
LASER CAT STARE
ACTIVATE!!

I'M THINKING OF HOW TO STEAL YOUR FOOD.

SOME DOGS SWIM . . .
AND THEN THERE'S KIBBLES.

No one sees me

in my cat fort.

DOGS ARE MAN'S BEST FRIEND?
YOU GOTTA BE KITTEN ME.

WHO SAID THEY COULD OUTRUN US? THAT KID OVER THERE?

I'M NOT MAD, I'M JUST HISS-APPOINTED

When your
best friend
picks someone
else for the
class project.

Again we see there is nothing you can possess which I cannot take away.

I found

a

CAAAAAAAAAT!!

BAD SELFIE.

Toucan play that game.

STOP COPYING ME. STOP COPYING ME. STOP COPYING ME. STOP COPYING M
STOP COPYING ME. STOP COPYING ME. STOP COPYING ME. STOP COPYING M
STOP COPYING ME. STOP COPYING ME. STOP COPYING ME. STOP COPYING M

STOP COPYING ME. STOP COPYING ME. STOP COPYING ME. STOP COPYING M
STOP COPYING ME. STOP COPYING ME. STOP COPYING ME. STOP COPYING M
STOP COPYING ME. STOP COPYING ME. STOP COPYING ME. STOP COPYING M

Because some ducks

KEEP OFF
THE GRASS!

just don't care.

Toto after the Wizard of Oz.

SNOW DOG HERE.

EVERY. MONDAY. MORNING.

WHEN DAD SAYS PIZZA'S FOR DINNER.

NO ONE MESSES WITH KITTY'S MILK.

NO ONE.

BAD SELFIE.

WHEN YOU THINK OF THE PERFECT JOKE,
BUT CAN'T SAY IT BECAUSE YOU'RE
LAUGHING SO HARD.

I'm flying to the MOOOooOOOoooOOOoooN!

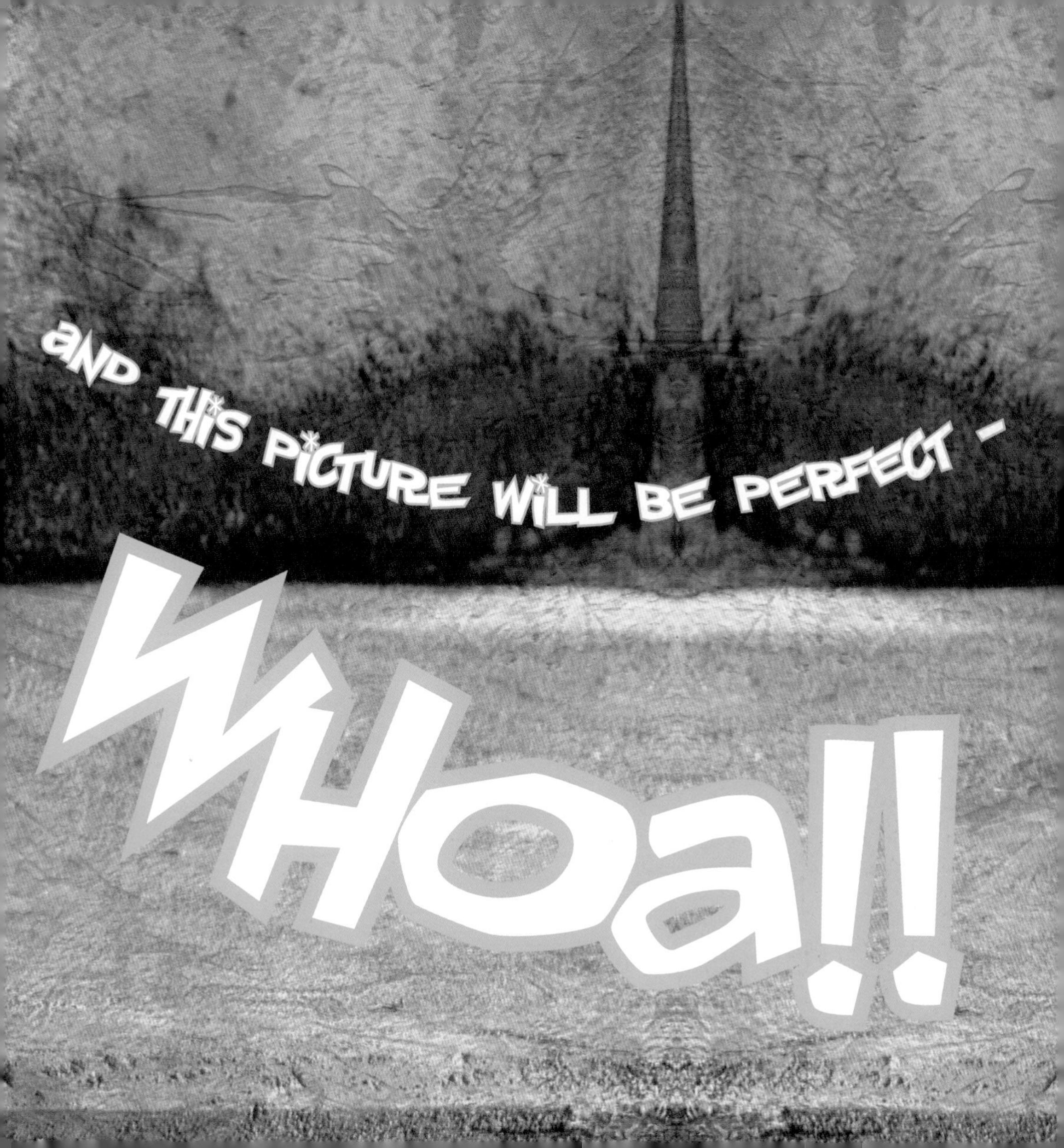
and this picture will be perfect –
WHOa!!

On the road of life, you must always remember to stop and smell the

BAAAAAAAAAAA.

NO.

Quietly plotting
EVIL PLANS.

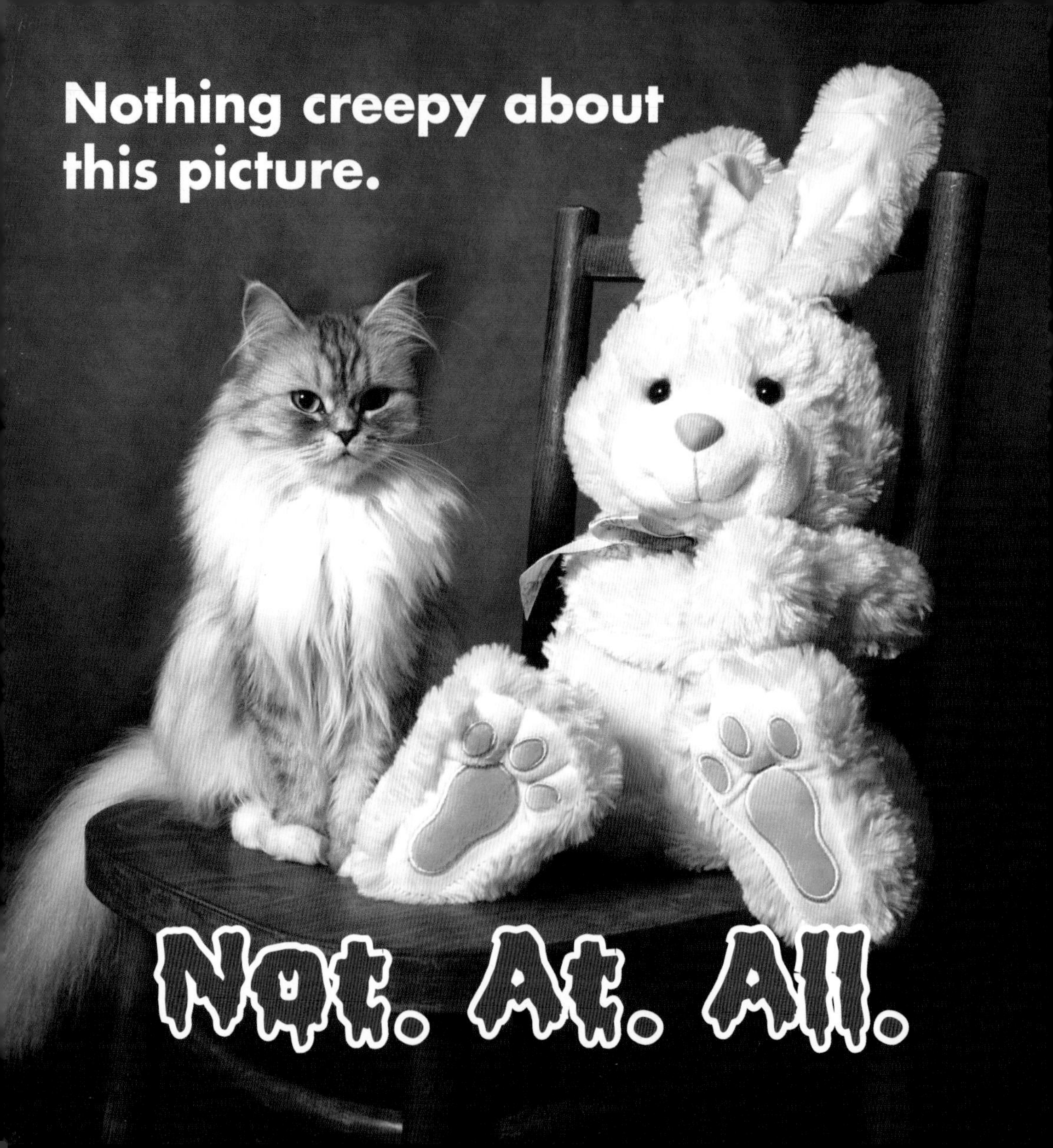
Nothing creepy about this picture.
Not. At. All.

I know what you're saying.

SO HOT.

SO COLD. SO GOOD.

Look at me. I'm a bee-you-tee-ful butterfly!